W9-BYY-058

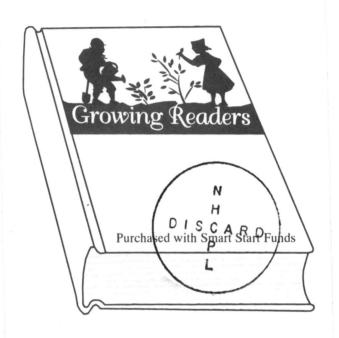

Growing Readers

Purchased with Smart Start Funds

Abraham Lincoln

by Lola M. Schaefer

Consulting Editor:
Gail Saunders-Smith, Ph.D.

Consultant:
Thomas F. Schwartz,
Illinois State Historian
Illinois Historic Preservation Society

Pebble Books
an imprint of Capstone Press
Mankato, Minnesota

Pebble Books are published by Capstone Press
818 North Willow Street, Mankato, Minnesota 56001
http://www.capstone-press.com

Library of Congress Cataloging-in-Publication Data
Schaefer, Lola M., 1950–
    Abraham Lincoln/by Lola M. Schaefer.
        p. cm.—(Famous Americans)
    Includes bibliographical references and index.
    Summary: Presents a brief biography of the country lawyer who became America's sixteenth
president and served during the Civil War.
    ISBN 0-7368-0108-1
    1. Lincoln, Abraham, 1809–1865—Juvenile literature. 2. Presidents—United States—
Biography—Juvenile literature. [1. Lincoln, Abraham, 1809–1865. 2. Presidents.] I. Title. II. Series.
E457.905.S33 1999
973.7'092—dc21   98-19962
[b]   CIP
                                                                  AC

Note to Parents and Teachers

This series supports national history standards by providing easy-to-read
biographies of people who had a great impact on history. This book describes
and illustrates the life of Abraham Lincoln, the 16th president of the United
States. The photographs support early readers in understanding the text.
Repetition of words and phrases helps early readers learn new words. This
book introduces early readers to vocabulary used in this subject area. The
vocabulary is defined in the Words to Know section. Early readers may need
assistance in reading some words and in using the Table of Contents, Words to
Know, Read More, Internet Sites, and Index/Word List sections of the book.

Table of Contents

4

Abraham Lincoln was born on February 12, 1809. People called him Abe. Abe grew up on a farm. Abe chopped wood and plowed fields.

Abe read many books. He read a book about George Washington. George was the first president of the United States. Abe liked George's ideas.

8

Abe and his family moved to Illinois in 1830. Abe worked many jobs. He was fair and kind. People called him Honest Abe.

Abe became a lawyer in 1836. He made plans to help the United States. Abe met Mary Todd. Mary liked Abe and his ideas. Abe married Mary on November 4, 1842.

12

Abe told people about his ideas. People in Illinois elected Abe to Congress. Abe worked hard in Washington, D.C.

14

Abe wanted all people to
be free. Some people
owned slaves. Slaves were
not free to choose their
homes or jobs. Abe wanted
to end slavery.

16

Many people liked Abe. He became the 16th president in 1861. Then the Civil War began. People in the North fought people in the South. They fought about slavery.

On the first day of January
in the year of our Lord one thousand
eight hundred and sixty-
three, all persons held as slaves
within the States in rebellion
against the United States
shall be thenceforward and forever free.

18

President Lincoln signed the Emancipation Proclamation in 1863. This paper set many slaves free. The Civil War ended two years later.

20

Some people were angry when the war ended. A man named John Wilkes Booth shot Abe. Abraham Lincoln died on April 15, 1865. The country was sad. People still remember today that President Lincoln helped to end slavery.

Words to Know

Civil War—the U.S. war fought between the Northern states and the Southern states; this war lasted from 1861 to 1865.

Congress—the government body of the United States that makes laws; Congress includes the Senate and the House of Representatives.

Emancipation Proclamation—an important paper Abraham Lincoln signed; this paper set many slaves free.

honest—a person who tells the truth is honest; people called Abraham Lincoln Honest Abe.

lawyer—a person who is trained to help people with the law; lawyers represent people who go to court.

plow—to prepare land for growing crops

slaves—people who are not free to choose their homes or jobs

Read More

Colver, Anne. *Abraham Lincoln: For the People.* A Discovery Biography. New York: Chelsea Juniors, 1992.

Mosher, Kiki. *Learning about Honesty from the Life of Abraham Lincoln.* A Character Building Book. New York: PowerKids Press, 1996.

Usel, T. M. *Abraham Lincoln: A Photo-Illustrated Biography.* Read and Discover Photo-Illustrated Biographies. Mankato, Minn.: Bridgestone Books, 1996.

Internet Sites

Abraham Lincoln
http://www.geocities.com/SunsetStrip/Venue/5217/lincoln.html

Abraham Lincoln Online
http://www.netins.net/showcase/creative/lincoln.html

The History Place Presents Abraham Lincoln
http://www.historyplace.com/lincoln/index.html

Index/Word List

Word Count: 235
Early-Intervention Level: 12

Editorial Credits
Michelle L. Norstad, editor; Clay Schotzko/Icon Productions, cover designer;
  Sheri Gosewisch, photo researcher

Photo Credits
Archive Photos, cover, 6, 12, 14, 16, 20
Corbis-Bettmann, 1, 10, 18
James P. Rowan, 8
Lincoln Boyhood National Memorial, 4

24